Sports Illustrated KIDS

THE SCIENCE OF BASEBALL

THE TOP 10 WAYS SCIENCE AFFECTS THE GAME

by Matt Chandler

Consultant:
Harold Pratt
President of Educational Consultants
Littleton, Colorado

CAPSTONE PRESS
a capstone imprint

Sports Illustrated KIDS Top 10 Science is published by Capstone Press,
1710 Roe Crest Drive, North Mankato, Minnesota 56003
www.mycapstone.com

Sports Illustrated Kids is a trademark of Time Inc. Used with permission.

Library of Congress Cataloging-in-Publication Data
Names: Chandler, Matt, author.
Title: The science of baseball : the top ten ways science affects the
game / by Matt Chandler.
Other titles: Top 10 Science. | Sports Illustrated kids (Capstone Press)
Description: North Mankato, Minnesota : Capstone Press, a Capstone
imprint, [2016] | Series: Top 10 Science | Series: Sports Illustrated
kids | Includes bibliographical references and index. | Audience: 8–10.
| Audience: 4 to 6.
Identifiers: LCCN 2015035088
ISBN 9781491482186 (library binding)
ISBN 9781491485989 (pbk.)
ISBN 9781491486023 (ebook pdf)
Subjects: LCSH: Baseball–Juvenile literature. | Sports sciences–
Juvenile literature.
Classification: LCC GV867.5 .C43 2016 | DDC 796.357–dc23
LC record available at http://lccn.loc.gov/2015035088

Editorial Credits
Adrian Vigliano, editor; Sarah Bennett, designer; Eric Gohl, media
researcher; Lori Blackwell, production specialist

Photo Credits
Dreamstime: Kmiragaya, 16; Eric Gohl: 14; Getty Images: MLB Photos/
Dan Donovan, 25 (all); Newscom: Icon Sportswire DDW/Kevin Sousa,
26-27, Icon Sportswire/Mark Goldman, 29, MCT/David Pokress,
9; Shutterstock: FADEDinkDesigns, 1, OZaiachin, 13 (bat); Sports
Illustrated: Al Tielemans, 19, Damian Strohmeyer, 10, David E. Klutho,
4–5, 21, 22, John Biever, 2, 8, John W. McDonough, 13, Robert Beck, cover,
7, Simon Bruty, 17

Design Elements: Shutterstock

Printed in the United States of America, in North Mankato, Minnesota.
112016   010160R

Table of Contents

From the mound, Los Angeles Dodgers pitcher Clayton Kershaw stares down at Miami Marlins outfielder Giancarlo Stanton. Will Kershaw light up the radar gun and blow a strike past Stanton? Or will Stanton connect with the fastball and drive it into the center field bleachers?

Baseball is a game of intense matchups as the best athletes square off in 162 battles each season. It takes more than ability to hit a baseball 400 feet or throw a fastball 95 miles per hour. You probably know about players' hard work, determination, and thousands of hours of practice. But science is another important key to every athlete's success on the field.

Why does the ball travel so far when Stanton makes contact? How does Kershaw throw the ball nearly 100 mph? Why are more home runs hit in Colorado than in Boston? You'll be amazed as you learn the science behind the game of baseball!

▲ Giancarlo Stanton

The Science Behind a Strike

Elite Arms

Some of the most powerful pitchers don't look like bodybuilders. Pedro Martinez, Randy Johnson, and Clayton Kershaw are all known as strikeout pitchers, yet physically, they don't look as muscular as some other players. So how are they able to make hitters look silly with their fastballs? You might think a pitcher's **velocity**, power, and control come from his arm. But it takes many parts of the body working together to deliver the perfect pitch.

A pitcher's arm, upper torso, and **pelvis** make partial rotations during every pitch. Each part must work in rhythm to generate **torque** before the pitch is released. From cocking his arm back to rotating his hips, the pitcher is building torque. He then pushes off the rubber, driving his weight toward home plate as he unleashes the pitch.

All of that twisting, turning, and motion comes together to create the force behind the pitch. It isn't just the muscles or size of the pitcher, it's his ability to harness the torque his body has created. The strongest arm in the game is ineffective if the pitcher can't make his entire body work to deliver the ball to the plate.

pelvis ⟹ the large bony structure near the base of the spine

torque ⟹ a force that causes objects to rotate

velocity ⟹ a measurement of both the speed and direction an object is moving rotate

◄ Pedro Martinez

Baseballs in Motion

English physicist Sir Isaac Newton is best known for his three laws of motion. These laws explain how forces affect objects. Newton's first law says that objects at rest stay at rest, and objects in motion stay in motion in a straight line unless an outside force acts on them. When applied to pitching, this means that a ball thrown straight will keep going straight until a force other than the one exerted by the pitcher moves it. When Newton made this discovery in 1686, baseball hadn't even been invented.

If a baseball could be thrown in a straight line, it would be much easier to hit. But there's no such thing as a straight pitch. As a ball flies through the air, outside forces act on it. Gravity constantly pulls down on the ball. As the ball spins, air pressure causes it to move or curve. Pitchers learn to work with these forces by controlling ball spin. This allows them to deliver pitches with extra movement or big curves. These pitches can be very hard to hit.

SCIENCE OF SAFETY

Imagine standing 60 feet away from Detroit Tigers pitcher Justin Verlander as he pitches you a fastball high and inside. Now imagine standing there without a batting helmet on! Batting helmets protect players from serious head injuries. But do you know how they work?

Most helmets are made from polycarbonate, a very light, incredibly strong plastic. When a ball hits the helmet, the energy from the ball is transferred to the helmet. Most of that energy is spread out through the helmet, minimizing the force to any one spot on the player's head. A player may still get a **concussion** after a beaning with a helmet on. But any injury will be much less severe than if he wasn't wearing a batting helmet.

◀ On average, about one player per game is hit by a pitch. Luckily most of these are not hits to a batter's head.

concussion ➡ an injury to the brain caused by a hard blow to the head

Swing for the Fences

When Boston Red Sox designated hitter David Ortiz crushes a home run, he makes it look easy. But hitting a baseball thrown at 90 miles per hour from nearly 60 feet away is incredibly difficult.

The human brain works like an incredible computer. The brain also determines whether a hitter strikes out or crushes a long ball. In only 125 milliseconds, Ortiz looks at a pitch, and his brain decides whether or not to swing. It then takes another 15 milliseconds for the brain to signal the muscles in the Ortiz's legs to begin the swing. From there, his brain signals the rest of the muscles in his pelvis, hips, and arms to go to work. Ortiz has to watch the pitcher with the ball in his hand. He then thinks about what pitch may be coming, and begins the process of swinging the bat. From when his hands begin to move, it is only 150 milliseconds until he hits, or misses, the pitch.

▼ David Ortiz uses strength, power, timing, and a great swing to crush a home run.

WHY IS THE SWEET SPOT SO SWEET?

Players talk about hitting the ball with a bat's sweet spot. It is said the ball travels farther and feels best coming off of this ideal spot on the bat. But why? The science of the sweet spot—also known as the center of percussion—has to do with **kinetic energy**.

If you've ever hit a ball off the end of a bat, especially in cold weather, you know how much it stings. It also usually isn't a very good hit. When the bat vibrates, it does more than sting your hands. It uses up valuable kinetic energy, leaving you with a weak hit. When the ball hits the sweet spot, much more kinetic energy is transferred into the ball, resulting in a better hit.

kinetic energy ➡ the energy in a moving object due to its mass and velocity

Angling for a Hit

The difference between grounding out to the shortstop and crushing a double to the gap can be a matter of inches. The pitcher is constantly changing his delivery just a little to gain an edge. The angle at which the ball leaves his hand determines the path it takes to the plate. Angles are crucial for hitters as well. If the batter drops his hands too low and swings at an upward angle, he could pop out. If he raises his hands and swings down on the ball, he risks grounding out.

One study determined the best launch angle for a home run is 45 degrees. But that doesn't account for wind, rain, humidity, bat speed, and other variables. The study, which looked at more than 500 home runs hit in a single month, showed the average swing angle was just 29 degrees.

The key to a great hit is to match the right swing angle with a pitch. Hitters who guess what pitch is coming have an advantage. So do hitters who can see the ball while it's still in the pitcher's hand. In both cases, the hitter gains a few extra milliseconds to adjust his swing.

BAT ANATOMY

Baseball bats are not all created equal. Bats differ depending on where the **mass** of the bat is distributed.

A power hitter will want a bat with a higher swing weight. A bat with a high swing weight will have a center of mass farther away from the handle. This bat will be harder to swing, but it will provide greater torque. A bat with the center of mass located closer to the handle will be easier to swing, but it will provide less torque.

▶ Mike Trout is considered one of the best hitters in baseball.

best home run launch angle = 45 degrees

45°

What's the best angle for hitting a home run?
One study determined the best angle to swing for a home run is 45 degrees.

mass ⇒ the amount of material in an object

13

The Air Effect

Coors Field, the home stadium of the Colorado Rockies, is a hitter's dream. In 2014 Coors Field was the only stadium in the majors where more than 200 home runs were hit. That's because Denver is about one mile above sea level. This means Denver's air is less dense than the air at sea level. Because air creates **friction** on a batted ball, a ball hit in less dense air faces less resistance and can travel farther.

A ball hit at sea level (in New York City, for example) that travels 400 feet could travel as much as 420 feet in Denver. What does the extra 20 feet mean for a hitter? If a ball loses just 1 percent of the distance it travels, the chance of hitting a home run drops by 7 percent!

Gravity is constantly pulling objects back to earth. When a batter makes contact with a pitch, the ball is launched into the air. But gravity is still pulling on the ball. In addition to gravity, factors such as air temperature and humidity have an effect on how far the ball travels.

◀ Coors Field, Denver, Colorado

---

friction ➡ the force created by a moving object as it rubs against a surface

Indoor Advantages

Do you think it would be easier to play baseball indoors without any weather elements? When playing outdoors, wind blowing toward the outfield is considered an advantage for hitters. But science may prove that theory wrong. Scientists studied how fly balls travel in every stadium in the majors and found that wind may not have as significant an effect on the flight of a ball as fans tend to think.

▲ Playing indoors can change the game by removing the effects of weather and sun glare.

Wind may not make a big difference, but indoors players don't have to worry about the sun. Some players say it is much harder to hit and catch outdoors during day games. The glare of the sun can make focusing on the ball more difficult.

"Eye black" is thought to help reduce the glare of the sun in a player's eyes. For decades, players have applied this grease, made of black charcoal, under their eyes. One study found that players who apply eye black have a "significant improvement" in glare reduction. But how does grease on your face keep the sun out of your eyes?

When light hits your skin, it can reflect up into your eyes, making things more difficult to see. But when wearing eye black, the grease absorbs some of the light and helps to reduce the reflection. As for the players wearing eye black on cloudy days, they're just trying to look cool.

▶ Washington Nationals outfielder Bryce Harper

17

Armed and Dangerous

Pitcher Power

Throwing a baseball is about two things: velocity and accuracy. But the science behind each throw changes between pitchers and fielders. We know that every ball is constantly pulled back toward the ground by gravity. We also know that friction slows down the ball. But what else impacts the velocity and accuracy of a throw?

Throwing from an elevated mound gives the pitcher added **momentum** as he delivers a pitch. Greater mound height helps add velocity to pitches and makes balls more difficult to hit. In 1969 Major League Baseball lowered the pitcher's mound from 15 inches (38.1 centimeters) high to its current level of 10 inches (25.4 cm). The league-wide batting average shot up 15 points that season as hitters could judge the natural drop of the ball better.

momentum ➡ a property of a moving object equal to its mass times its velocity

The pitcher stands on the mound, at the pitching rubber. To deliver a pitch, he goes through a series of basic steps designed to generate force that can be transferred into the ball. The pitcher has to use his hips, torso, arm, and legs to deliver the perfect pitch. Once he has all of that working, the final step is delivery. The rubber allows the pitcher to drive off with his back foot and use that momentum to add velocity to each pitch.

▼ Kansas City Royals pitcher Jeremy Guthrie uses the mound to his advantage when delivering a pitch.

Arcs in the Outfield

For fielders, especially outfielders, throwing is all about launch angle. In a game in 2014, Oakland Athletics outfielder Yoenis Cespedes hurled the ball about 318 feet in time to beat a runner to the plate. Cespedes' perfect throw to the catcher saved a run.

Watching the flight path of his throw offers a lesson in launch angle. Unlike a pitcher, who throws the ball at a very low angle, Cespedes threw the ball with a big, high arc. His throw was estimated to have traveled at more than 95 mph. But he had to throw it more than five times the distance from the pitching rubber to home plate.

Working against gravity, an outfielder has to adjust his throw to make it high enough to reach the intended target.

HORNSBY

▶ St. Louis Cardinals left fielder Matt Holliday knows how to adjust the arc of his throw to deliver the ball to the infield as quickly as possible.

The ball's path creates an arc.

SMITH 2 SCHOENDIENST BUCK

38

The Perfect Bunt

There's more to a bunt than holding out the bat. Every good bunt involves reducing the energy of the ball after it hits the bat.

If a bunting batter lines up the bat and simply holds it still, the ball will hit the bat and bounce away. But this bunt will probably reach a fielder quickly, and the batter will likely be thrown out. Instead, bunters try to slow the ball. They wait until just before the ball makes contact with the bat, then pull back the bat head slightly. This absorbs more of the energy of the pitch and "deadens" the ball. A deadened bunt will travel less distance and take longer to reach the fielders.

But a deadened bunt is only half the battle. A slow bunt that travels right back toward the pitcher will probably result in an out. A batter must use angles to his advantage. The player needs to angle his bat to direct the bunt either left or right. He also needs to make contact with the lower part of the bat barrel. This way the bunt is angled toward the ground instead of up in the air, where it could be caught for an easy out. The perfect bunt is one where the ball is deadened, angled down to the ground, and directed between the pitcher and third baseman or first baseman. By splitting the defenders, the batter increases his chances of making it safely to first base.

◄ Kansas City Royals center fielder Lorenzo Cain pulls his bat to bunt the ball at a downward angle.

Stealing Science

Hall of Fame outfielder Rickey Henderson played in the majors for 25 years. He stole 1,406 bases in his career—a major league record. Henderson was fast, but he was also smart. He knew the science of sliding and earned many of his stolen bases with the fast-but-risky headfirst slide.

Sliding headfirst may help a runner reach the base slightly faster than a feet-first slide. The reason has to do with a player's **center of gravity**. The center of gravity varies from one person to another, but it is always somewhere in the lower abdomen. Whether the player slides feet-first or headfirst, the center of gravity will move forward with the velocity and momentum the player had when he began sliding.

In a headfirst slide, the player generates extra momentum by launching his center of gravity forward. Sliding feet first offers slightly less momentum as the player is simply dropping his center of gravity to the ground. Also, a feet-first slide may create more friction than a headfirst slide and result in slightly slower movement.

center of gravity ➡ the point around which an object's weight is evenly distributed

▲ Rickey Henderson launched his center of gravity forward to give himself the best chance of reaching home plate safely.

Grass or Turf?

In 1966 the Houston Astrodome became the first Major League Baseball stadium to use artificial turf. By 1970 six teams had installed artificial turf. Many more teams followed in the 1970s and early 1980s. Today only two stadiums in the majors still use artificial turf: the Tampa Bay Rays' Tropicana Field and the Toronto Blue Jays' Rogers Centre. So what's the difference between playing on grass or turf?

▼ Diving onto a modern turf field, such as Toronto's Rogers Centre, can cause an upward spray of rubber pellets.

The biggest difference between turf and grass is ball movement. The ball travels much faster and farther on artificial turf as opposed to natural grass. There are many factors that affect the velocity of the ball once it hits the ground. Natural grass and dirt absorb more of a ball's energy and cause it to slow down more quickly. Grass also creates more friction, which slows down ball movement. The opposite is true for turf fields. Today's artificial fields are filled with rubber pellets in between the blades of "grass." The rubber acts like a spring when the ball hits it and allows the ball to travel with more velocity and momentum.

A ball traveling faster can mean a double to the gap that would have been a single on grass. But it can also mean a ball reaches the outfielder so fast the base runners can't advance as far.

10

Follow the Bouncing Ball

Shortstop is one of the most demanding positions for a fielder. Baltimore Orioles shortstop J. J. Hardy won three consecutive Gold Gloves from 2012 to 2014 as the best defensive shortstop in the American League. But sometimes even Hardy has trouble fielding a wildly bouncing ball.

A pitcher creates spin by how he holds the ball and how he releases it during the pitch. The batter swings and more spin is created as the ball leaves the bat. Once a baseball hits the ground, it can behave unpredictably. The ball may take a bad bounce over a fielder's glove. Sometimes a ball with lots of topspin even appears to pick up speed once it hits the ground.

Infielders have to be ready for any bounces a ball may take. When a ball is hit toward Hardy, he tracks the ball and begins moving to his right or left in a split second. If the ball is coming right at him, he will probably charge forward to grab it as quickly as possible. If he can't reach the ball running, he must decide if a diving catch is necessary. No matter what, his goal is always to get to the ball as quickly as possible to allow the most time to deliver a throw and get an out.

◀ J. J. Hardy has to stay
focused when he tracks
a ball in the infield.

Whether it's a home-run-crushing batter or a fireballing
pitcher, baseball superstars all rely on science as part of their
on-field success. Each throw, hit, and slide is both a skill and
a science. So the next time you're watching your favorite team
take the field, consider the science behind their success!

GLOSSARY

center of gravity (SEN-tur UHV GRAV-uh-tee) ⟶ the point around which an object's weight is evenly distributed

concussion (kuhn-KUH-shuhn) ⟶ an injury to the brain caused by a hard blow to the head

friction (FRIK-shuhn) ⟶ the force created by a moving object as it rubs against a surface

kinetic energy (ki-NET-ik EN-ur-jee) ⟶ the energy in a moving object due to its mass and velocity

mass (MASS) ⟶ the amount of material in an object

momentum (moh-MEN-tuhm) ⟶ a property of a moving object equal to its mass times its velocity

pelvis (PEL-viss) ⟶ the large bony structure near the base of the spine where the legs attach

torque (TORK) ⟶ a force that causes objects to rotate

velocity (vuh-LOSS-uh-tee) ⟶ a measurement of both the speed and direction an object is moving

READ MORE

Chandler, Matt. *Who's Who of Pro Baseball: A Guide to the Game's Greatest Players.* North Mankato, Minn.: Capstone Press, 2016.

Drier, David. *The Science of Baseball with Max Axiom, Super Scientist.* North Mankato, Minn.: Capstone Press, 2015.

Hantula, Richard. *Science at Work in Baseball.* New York: Marshall Cavendish Benchmark, 2012.

INTERNET SITES

FactHound offers a safe, fun way to find Internet sites related to this book. All of the sites on FactHound have been researched by our staff.

Here's all you do:

Visit *www.facthound.com*

Type in this code: 9781491482186

Check out projects, games and lots more at
www.capstonekids.com

INDEX